Happy Birthday, Catherine.

Dot Muise

Dot is a long time friend
and Music Director
at the UU of
Ft. Lauderdale —

hope you enjoy her
Mother's poems !

Love,
Aunt Debbi
4-21-97

SINGING HEART

SINGING HEART

The Poems of
Florence Brigham Matthews

Compiled by Dorothy R. Muise

Illustrated by Deborah J. Muise

VANTAGE PRESS
New York / Los Angeles / Chicago

In loving memory of my mother, FBM (1898–1978)
—*Dorothy R. Muise*

Contents

Part Seven. Songs of Sadness

Part Eight. Just Poems

Acknowledgment

This collection of poetry is published to fulfill a wish to preserve for her children, grandchildren, and future generations, the beautiful expression of joy in living of Florence Brigham Matthews.

SINGING HEART

Part One

Songs to Nature

Autumn Is Coming

Autumn is coming! I heard it today;
Honk of the wild geese over the bay;
Far to the southland and sunshine they fly,
"Autumn is coming!" I hear in their cry.

Autumn is coming! I saw it today,
Painting the foliage brilliantly gay,
Scarlet and amber and crimson and gold.
Autumn is coming! The year's growing old.

Autumn is coming! I felt it today;
Knew that the summer was passing away;
Lingered, reluctant to bid it good-bye—
Autumn is coming, and summer must die.

Three Goddesses
(May 1, 1918)

Three goddesses, and each unlike the other:
Dawn, Day, and Night; and all so wondrous fair.
I worship them with eyes and heart aflame,
And long to touch them, though I do not dare.

Dawn has a body all of rose and gold,
The first gray mist of morning in her eyes,
Sunlight enmeshed within her shining hair,
Youth on her lips, and Love, and Paradise.

Day is a flame, a joy-abounding life,
Crowned with a burnished copper aureole,
Blue-brilliant, cloudless heaven in her eyes,
And laughter shining from her vivid soul.

Night is a graceful-gliding shadow queen,
With velvet eyes grown soft with wistful dreams,
And dusk-veiled crown, which shimmers through the
    gloom,
Set with still-shining stars, and soft moonbeams.

Three goddesses, and each unlike the other:
Dawn, Day, and Night; and all so wondrous fair.
I watch with adoration in my heart,
And long to tell my love, but do not dare.

Tornado

A savage beast with a vicious eye
Unleashing its wicked wrath.
A swirling funnel of wind
Traveling a random path.
Screaming and spinning
And twisting its way
Killing and leaving
Its dead for decay.
Extensive in
Destruction
Its fury
Is brief
Leaving
Its mark
A scar
That i$_s$
$g_{r_{i_{e_{f_!}}}}$

Majestic Tree

Knotted and gnarled
Its wooden tentacles winding upward.
Silent in grandeur,
Standing alone.
A firm foundation of fibrous fingers
Supporting a body ringed with age.
The wisdom of decades
Locked in each pulpy vein.

To an Eastern Lily
(*July 8, 1917*)

O strange, exotic flower, with your last breath
You breathe out perfume on the ravished air,
And even as your flaming petals fall,
And leave the white-gold heart of you so bare,
Your flaunting beauty challenges cold Death;
Your scarlet gleams upon the dewy ground—
In red-gold brilliance flashes on the sight
Like some brown, wrinkled woman, jewel-crowned.
Strange flower, that blooms and dies, unconquered still,
Flame-tipped, triumphant in your last, mad hour,
So may my soul, unconquered, meet pale Death
In beauty-flame like yours, most beauteous flower.

Night Song

Upon the way where newly fallen snow
Lies glistening, white and soft, my feet must go;
No moon to light my way, no friendly star
    To glow afar.

Before me, beckoning into the night,
The snowy pathway, strangely, dimly white;
On either side the phantom shapes of pine
    In stately line.

Black shadows where the velvet darkness sleeps,
And where an inky brook in silence sweeps;
A gentle breeze that sighs across the hill
    And then is still.

Vague whispers—rustling noises in the dark—
Then hush again, and silence soft, till—hark!
It is my own heart calling to the night
    In sheer delight.

One Summer Day

The sun was a flaming marigold;
The sky was a turquoise blue;
And the sun shone bright on the grassy height
Where the daisy blossoms grew.

The breeze was a fairy's perfumed breath;
The birds were a heavenly choir;
And the big gray stone was a royal throne
In the midst of a world empire.

The king was a regal youth and brave;
The queen was a maiden fair;
And the wind brushed by with a whispered sigh,
As he kissed them, and left them there.

Their youth was a gladsome, fearless thing;
Their love was a song of May;
And the world was glad for the lass and lad
In the glow of that summer day.

Break, Waves!
(September 1, 1917)

Break, waves, in restless grandeur on the shore;
My heart is restless, and my eager ear;
I love to listen to your mighty roar.
    Break, waves, and let me hear!

Break, waves, and toss the tangled seaweed high.
Your foaming crests are snowy plumes to me;
They picture triumph, freedom to my eye.
    Break, waves, and let me see!

Break, waves, in sullen anger and unrest;
Break o'er me, as within your power I kneel.
I love your chilling surge against my breast.
    Break, waves, that I may feel!

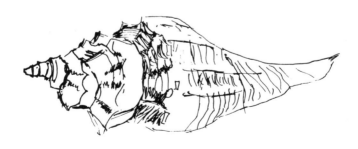

Beauty
(*September 1, 1917*)

We're riding through the woods and hills and down beside
    the sea,
And all the world is beautiful, a wonderland to me:
The yellow of the goldenrod that's just begun to bloom;
The flashing of a red-winged bird across the woodland
    gloom;
A field of golden buttercups; the scent of new-turned hay;
The glitter of the sunlight on the blueness of the bay;
The perfume of the ripened grapes; a bird's defiant scream;
The lush grass of the marshland; or a little inland stream;
The rush of wind against my cheek; our swift and steady
    glide;
The wonder at the beauty that the turn ahead may hide—
There's beauty, beauty, beauty here in everything for me;
For all the world's a wonderland to smell and hear and see.

Part Two

Songs of Love

The Rendezvous
(July 26, 1918)

Love and I had a rendezvous.
We were a joyous pair;
I was careless and Love was bold;
I was youth, but ah, Love was old!
(Strange indeed was the tale he told!)
Love and I had a rendezvous,
But Love was never there.

Love Disguised
(June 28, 1918)

Love does not come to me with laughing eyes
And joyous heart, and in a merry guise;
Raise high the cup and call, "Come! Taste and see
How wonderful the wine of Love may be!"

Love comes to me with thoughtful, downbent head,
Perplexed and saddened with an unknown dread;
And for my heart to feed upon brings tears
And shame; Love like a mockery appears.

Is Love then joy and sweetness—or distress?
Put off the mask, and give me happiness!

Love Unexpressed
(March 6, 1918)

I love you so! But you do not know,
For my quiet heart is still;
I can't express what you will not guess,
For my tongue denies my will.

I lift my eyes, but you tantalize
With your heart that cannot see;
And my wistful gaze for an answer prays,
But you have no glance for me.

To have a friend to the very end
Is what you might require.
You're kind to me, but you do not see
That your love is my desire.

I want your smile for myself a while,
And the pressure of your hand.
I love you so! But you do not know,
And you will not understand.

The Princess and the Peasant Maid

He's told her that he loves her;
He's told the same to me—
It was his heart proclaimed it,
That earnest passion-plea.

He kisses her and loves her,
And then my lips he'll seek;
My arms and my embraces;
His kiss upon my cheek.

He flatters her and woos her
And smiles into her eyes;
But I have seen him tremble—
His boyish color rise.

And I have felt his heart beat
So fast against my breast!
'Tis rumored he will wed her—
I know he loves me best.

But she has golden treasure;
Her rank and name are high;
No wealth my hands are holding;
A nameless maid am I.

Though she may have him near her,
Though he and I must part,
His life, his thought, his longings
Are mine—I hold his heart!

I Love You

I love you
Not so much in those moments when desire
Sweeps me, all breathless, into your embrace;
Nor yet when banter on our lips is gay
And laughter lights your face;
Nor even when your fingers touch the keys
And seem to play upon my very heart;
But in those fleeting moments when I glimpse
Your soul behind the mask that keeps apart
Even the nearest of us. Only then
My soul draws near to yours, and I can feel
I see and know you—and we understand.
Only such rare sweet moments may reveal—
I love you!

Three Wooings
(January 26, 1920)

"I love you!" said his smiling lips
  With light and shallow tone.
How could he tell me of a love
  His heart had never known?

"I want you," said his claiming kiss,
  That bound my spirit's wings;
But he could only give me love
  That seeks the dross of things.

I need you!" and your soul's deep dream
  Is shining in your eyes.
"Oh take me, Love, and keep me, Love!"
  My singing heart replies.

Unsatisfied

How can dream kisses satisfy my heart,
That treasures vivid memories of you?
Your ardent eyes—your eager mouth—your arms
Holding me close and closer! Was it true—
That sweet desire—that aching ecstasy—
That surge of pounding pulses we both knew?

I sleep—I dream—I wake, and cry to you
Across the miles that keep us far apart.
Beloved, do you hear? I want you so!
But Echo answers, mocking, as I start
And tremble—listening for your voice anew.
How can dream kisses satisfy my heart?

My Lady

Soft as the feathery fleece of a cloud bank;
Fine as a spider-web snare;
Made to entangle my quivering heartstrings—
    That is your shimmering hair.

Deep as some pool in the heart of the woodland;
Blue as the midsummer skies;
Bright as twin stars in the shine of the moonlight—
    Those are your glorious eyes.

Color of dawn and the flush of the morning;
Texture of blossoming pear;
Fragrance of trailing arbutus in Springtime—
    Never a cheek was more fair.

Tint of a scarlet-plumed tanager feather—
Sweets that the butterfly sips;
Swinging on heavy-hung clusters of roses,
    Never so sweet as your lips.

Graceful as lilies abloom in the Springtime;
Light as a dragonfly's wing;
Fair as a midsummer day at its dawning—
    That is the maiden I sing.

To H. H. M.

I love the wondrous glory of your hair,
A crown of burnished copper, and your eyes—
They are so clear and blue; I love their glance,
Honest, direct, merry, and frank, and true;
(Such eyes could never lie). I love your lips;
Your smile, your laughter, and yourself, my queen;
But you, you do not know
    I love you so!

I love your body, for my eyes delight
To look at you and worship; and I love
The mind, the heart, the wondrous soul of you,
Which smiles upon your lips and in your eyes.
I know that you are very wonderful
To me, and that you own my heart, my queen;
But you—you do not know
    I love you so!

Confession

I wonder what you'd think, if you could know
How I admire the mind and heart of you!
If you could feel the fluttering of my soul
When you are near! I wonder if you knew
How, when your eyes met mine, my heartstrings sang;
And did you see me flush? I know you smiled;
I wondered if you thought—what did you think?
You could not dream of anything so wild
As that I love you, for it is not so!
I harbor no such foolish, empty dream;
But when I hear your voice, it makes me glad,
And things are not exactly as they seem.
I might have loved you, had you not a wife,
Whose every thought in partnership you share,
And had you lived your youth a bit before,
Or I a little later; all I dare
Is just to let my heart admire your brain,
Your body, and your soul—the power of you;
And that is all—and yet—it isn't all!
I wonder what you'd think now, if you knew!

Meeting Again

You whom I almost love against my will,
Bringer of things forgotten and gone by,
Strange that my heart should feel the old sweet thrill,
Meeting again the glance of your blue eye.

You whom I loved and lost so long ago,
Herald of memories of smiles and tears,
Strange that my tongue in greeting falters so,
After the parting and the lapse of years.

You whom I thought I had forgotten quite,
Now that you smile and take me by the hand,
Strange that my fingers falter, as in fright!
What does it mean? Dear, do you understand?

On the Fence

We sat upon the fence rail
  A good three feet apart;
But who could guess the longings
  That fluttered in each heart?

For all we were so silent,
  So strangely stiff and shy,
A thousand things unuttered
  Were mirrored in each eye.

We swung our feet and wriggled,
  And whispered in the dark,
And watched a firefly glitter,
  A flashing, lonesome spark.

The moon was shining on us
  A spell we'd never known,
We couldn't understand it—
  'Twas good to be alone.

Just boy and girl together,
  A strangely happy pair,
We sat upon the fence rail,
  And found contentment there.

An Old Story

A fool there was, and she loved a man,
As fools have done since the world began.
She loved his hair, and she loved his eyes;
He filled her soul with a glad surprise;
She loved his smile, and she loved his tone;
She loved the man for himself alone.
But he had a wife, and he loved her, too,
So what was the lovelorn fool to do?
She gave no thought to that wife he had;
She loved the man—and she called him "Dad!"

Part Three

Songs of Faith

An Ideal of Life

To help someone live better day by day;
To show some soul just how to find God's way;
To walk so that another's feet may tread
The selfsame path, and follow where I led,
And see the Savior at the journey's end;
To be to everyone I meet a friend;
The weary burden from some heart to lift;
In darkest clouds to find one little rift;
To bring a smile to someone's tired eyes;
To hopeless lips, a laugh in place of sighs;
To make a song in someone's weary heart;
Wherever I may be to do my part
To make this old world better, and to live
As best I can; give all I have to give
Of love and service; and, whate'er betide,
To follow to the end with God as guide.

What's the Use?

What's the use of hopin',
When tomorrow never comes?
What's the use of tryin',
When cold Fate's turned down his thumbs?
What's the use of prayin',
When God somehow never hears?
What's the use of livin',
When life holds so many tears?

What's the use of frettin',
When it only makes you blue?
What's the use of idlin',
When there's lots o' work to do?
What's the use of cryin',
When a laugh will lighten care?
What's the use of failin',
When God always answers prayer?

Poor Little Soul!

Poor little soul, you are so very small
  In this vast world of ours!
The days, the weeks, the months, the years go on
  With sun and showers—

Poor little soul! What matter if you fail
  And miss your chosen way?
What matter if you stumble in the dark,
  And go astray?

Poor little soul, so insignificant;
  So hard the constant fight!
What use to live? What loss to die;
  And gain eternal night?

Poor little soul, the world has passed you by,
  Unheeding your despair.
What matter if you fail? The world won't know,
  But God will care!

A Mother's Thanksgiving Prayer

I know that all my blessings, Lord,
From Thy great bounty come;
I thank Thee, Father, for the Love
Which makes my house a home.

I thank Thee for the common tasks,
Which daily must be met;
They make so sweet the hour of ease
Which comes when sun is set.

I thank Thee for my little ones;
For friends who hold me dear;
For Hope that lights the forward way;
For laughter—and a tear.

I thank Thee for the harder things—
The care and bitter pain,
Which teach my heart to turn to Thee
Its courage to regain.

And though I cannot understand
The heartache and the loss,
I know whatever is—is best,
And thank Thee for the cross.

Crosses

She loved her husband dearly; they had lived
Together happily for many years;
Yet, when he died, she bowed her lovely head
In resignation, smiling through her tears.
"The Lord has giv'n—the Lord takes back again—
And blessed be His holy Name. Amen."

Fate robbed her of the riches long enjoyed;
Her poor hands found strange tasks that they must do;
And still she lifted high her gallant head;
No bitterness her soaring spirit knew.
"The Lord has giv'n—the Lord takes back again—
And blessed be His holy Name. Amen."

Age set his ugly seal upon her face,
Robbing her of all beauty; and men's eyes
No longer followed warmly as she passed;
And women gazed no more with envious sighs.
Then rose to Heav'n at last her anguished pray'r—
"God, let me die! This cross I cannot bear!"

Part Four
Songs of War

The World Is at War

The world is at war; we are fighting our brothers,
Land against land, and sea against sea;
While horror is gripping the world with its madness,
The devil is laughing in hideous glee.

Land against land we are striving in agony;
Fighting for country, honor, and right;
While Sorrow is weeping in passionate sadness,
The devil is laughing in fiendish delight.

The world is at war, and the earth is a battlefield
Soaked with the blood of the brave who have fought.
While Death is abroad, and destruction is raging,
The devil is laughing at what he has wrought.

How Long, O Lord?

How long, O Lord, must the cloud of war
Hang darkly threatening o'er Thy land?
How long, O Lord, must the battle cry
Reecho loudly from strand to strand?
Until the earth is a desert waste?
Until the ocean is choked with dead?
Until the world is a lifeless thing?
Until the heaven itself is red?

How long, O Lord, e'er the shout be stilled,
And the strife be o'er, and the carnage cease?
How long, O Lord, e'er we live again
In the blessed safety of rest and peace?
Until the good has been lost in shame?
Until the strong and the weak shall blend
In one great river of lifeblood red?
How long, O Lord, or is this the end?

I Am Afraid!

I am afraid, for I hear the drums,
Beating the march for the men today,
Hearing the crowd as it cheers them on
I am afraid he will go away.

I am afraid he will go to war,
Marching away in a soldier suit,
Marching away to the throbbing drum,
Steady of eye and firm of foot.

I am afraid he will fight—and oh!
Fall and die for his country's name,
Me afar, while he lies in death!
Nothing ever can be the same!

I am afraid he will go—and still,
What if his heart should fear the sword?
What if he shrink and turn aside?
I am afraid—afraid! Oh, God!

The Beast

The air is the haunt of the Demons of Darkness
Who bring with them horror, destruction, and dread;
The earth is a slaughterhouse heaped with the dying;
The sea is a burial place for the dead.

And Death, like a monster that's ever insatiate,
Is gaping his jaws with a hideous grin;
While blood is adrip from the tongue he is lolling,
Awaiting the feast we are flinging within.

The air is the haunt of the vulture and raven;
The earth the delight of the wolf and the worm;
The shark is askulk in the depths of the ocean;
The beast is the victor; he only is firm!

War

Was it a dream? I fancied that I heard
Hoofbeat and drumbeat, and the beat of hearts,
Throbbing in gripping horror—silent fear;
I thought I heard the tread of many feet:
The tread of horse and man—the tread of Death;
I thought I heard the scream of shot and shell;
The scream of dying human, dying beast—
And at the sound my blood grew cold and chill,
Curdled and froze within me, and my heart
Shuddered and shivered from that shriek of pain.
It is too horror full to be a dream,
Too horror full to be reality;
It is the madness of a crooked brain;
It is the phantom of a fancy crazed.
War! It is not of Earth or Heaven born,
But of the demon fantasies of Hell!

Part Five
Songs to the Children

A Mother's Cry

Sob, winds, sob and sigh.
Shrieking, moaning, sorrowful, wild!
Wail, winds, your despairing cry—
    Gone! My child! My child!

Weep, clouds, and weep, sky,
Grieving darkly, and full of woe!
My fount of tears is long-since dry—
    Weep, my grief to show!

Mourn, earth, let joy die!
Happiness in my world is done.
Shout, all things, with a last, wild cry—
    Dead! My son! My son!

Maternity

After the agony of pain
My heart such triumph owns!
But just across the hall from me
An unwed mother moans.

My baby nestles at my breast;
My eyes are full of dreams;
But just across the hall from me
The unwed mother screams.

What if it were my little girl,
Who now so sweetly sleeps?
My heart lifts up a prayer to God.
The unwed mother weeps.

My Son

When he's awake he is a MAN
So big and rough and strong—
A pirate fierce—a soldier brave—
A robber living in a cave—
The sheriff, capturing some knave—
A hero—right or wrong!

A man can't kiss and hug and such;
He's far too big for loving—much.

When he's asleep he's just my boy
So cuddly warm and sweet.
His hair a mop of silken curls,
His cheek all rosy like a girl's—
His fist, which such defiance hurls,
Relaxed upon the sheet.

By day so far away is he!
At night my babe comes back to me.

Love Cycle

(Written by a grandmother one month before the birth of her first grandchild.)

Life filled my cup of love
Right to the brim.
I drank its every drop—
The glad—the grim.

I gave a son to life;
A daughter, too.
From their full chalices
I drank anew.

My daughter's daughter smiles;
Another cup
Of brimming life and love
Is filling up.

yuck!

To Martha
(On the death of a grandchild.)

Our blossom dropped ere yet she came to flower.
We miss her sore; but gentle, pitying Time
Holds out her healing hands in this sad hour
To ease our stricken hearts. The silver chime
Of childish laughter echoes sweetly yet;
Her graceful hands—her silken hair of gold—
She is not dead whose loved ones ne'er forget;
She lives forevermore—just four years old.

The Life Worthwhile

Ironing little rompers,
Mending little socks,
Washing grimy faces,
Combing tangled locks,

Teaching lips to prattle
Prayers in baby talk,
Guiding little footsteps,
Learning how to walk—

Some may call it drudging;
Shirk it with a smile;
But I call it LIVING;
That's the life worthwhile.

The Coming of Santa Claus

Snow asparkle in the treetops;
Snow agleam upon the ground;
Stars atwinkle in the moonlight,
Shedding softest light around.

Hush of waiting—tingling silence—
Secrets borne upon the breeze,
As it whispers slyly, softly,
Through the heavy-laden trees.

Lad asleep upon his pillow,
Dreaming dreams of wild delight.
Jolly moon is smiling broadly;
Santa Claus will come tonight.

Hark! a noise upon the housetop—
Chime of bells in tinkling tune;
Stamp of reindeer hoofs impatient;
No one sees but Mr. Moon.

Down the chimney softly stealing,
Untold treasures on his back,
Santa Claus, the jolly fellow,
Brings the wonders of his pack.

Now he stands beside the fireplace,
Finds the stocking hung with care,
Fills it full of toys and goodies,
Overflowing, generous share.

Tiptoe to the little dreamer;
Tuck his straying curls aside;
Smile and turn away, Old Santa;
Vanish up the chimney wide.

When the brightness of the sunshine
Wakes the laddie with its beam
To the joys that Santa brought him,
Who would tell him 'twas a dream?

World Sympathy

(Written on the kidnapping of the Lindbergh baby.)

The news flashed forth upon the startled air;
And the world heard—aghast—
Our Lindy's baby stolen from his bed!
A shadow overcast
All hearts and homes; and every mother prayed
Holding her own babe near;
And every father felt within his breast
The clutch of fear.

And children pausing in their merry play,
Stood hushed and awed.
A whole world breathless, raised its myriad prayer
To an all-pitying God.

Part Six
Songs to Friends and Neighbors

Neighbors

My neighbor's house is roomy;
It boasts a servants' hall.
My own two hands must serve me;
My home is small.

My neighbor has no babies;
No household cares to fret.
But I have two small people
And meals to get.

My neighbor's face is lovely,
Her raiment rich and new.
I've little time for mirrors;
My clothes are few.

My neighbor's throat is jeweled,
And orchids deck her frocks;
But Sonny brings me violets,
Or hollyhocks.

In love and sweet contentment
I'm richer far than she;
I pity my poor neighbor—
She pities me!

My Neighbor

I had not known her very well,
Although she lived quite near.
I thought of her as "nice enough,
But just a little queer."
And then the other night we met
And walked our way together,
Beginning, as is usual—
By chatting of the weather.
But ere we said a gay goodnight
At our respective goals,
We'd touched on music and the arts
And our immortal souls;
And why a certain doctor has
So fine a reputation—
The education of our sons—
And just what ails the nation.
And I was much surprised to find
Our judgements so agree.
I know my neighbor better now.
She's very much like me!

To One Who Understood
(October 10, 1917)

You understood! I had not cried before,
But when you came in silent sympathy,
And put your arms about me with no word,
You do not know what comfort came to me.

Another would have spoken or consoled;
They only hurt who do not comprehend;
But oh, the joy of love that feels and knows.
The wonder of an understanding friend!

To Peg

My Peg, I cannot bear to see you cry;
I love you so, my dear, it hurts my heart
To see the lonesome teardrops in your eyes;
It seems as if I must have failed, somehow—
Have failed in love, although I love so well.
You know I love you—worship you—would give
The little all I have to make you glad;
And yet, you are not happy—have I failed?
My Peg, I cannot bear to see you cry!

When you are sad, I long to comfort you,
To put my arms around you—with my love
Enfold you and protect you from all pain.
I long to say the word to comfort you;
The word to check your tears, and make you smile;
To bring the sunshine to your face again.
When you are sad, I long to comfort you!

And yet, I cannot somehow understand,
For all my love, the way to reach your heart—
The way to teach you all my love for you—
The way to comfort when your heart is sad.
The others know; I do not understand.
They come and love you, and I stand aside
And watch them—and their word of comfort brings
A solace that my silent sympathy
Can never bring—and yet—I love you so!
I wish that I, like them, could understand!

To a Friend Going Away
(*March 6, 1918*)

You go away today,
And hearts are lonely that you leave behind.
Strange what a difference one such life can make,
And one such mind!

You go away today,
And hearts are heavy as they say goodbye.
And there is no one here who'll miss you more,
Perhaps, than I.

Thought Messages

Call to me now, with your wealth of devotion
Still all unchanging, as deep and as strong
Over the miles that are stretching between us,
Over the years that have parted us long.

Call to me now, and my spirit will answer you,
Bridging the distance as though it were nought;
Only remember me—then I shall fly to you,
Borne on the wings of your wandering thought.

Oh, for One Moment!

Oh, for one moment I could call my own—
To fold my hands, to close my tired eyes;
To sit before the fire and idly dream.
Oh, for one moment just to be alone!
To take no thought of how that moment flies,
But just to drift a little down life's stream,
Forgetting care, forgetting everything,
And letting all the song that's in me sing.

Oh, for one moment in the round of days,
When time was all my own, a little while
To sit and dream as I would like to do,
To call to mind your well-remembered ways;
To see again the gladness of your smile.
Oh, for one moment—just to dream of you!

But on and on and on my heart must go;
There is no time to dream—life wills it so.

Part Seven
Songs of Sadness

Sorrow's Recompense

'Tis only he whose grief has been so deep
That he has almost lost the power to feel;
'Tis only he whose wound has been so wide
That even Time can never wholly heal;

'Tis only he whose pain has seared and burned
Until the fount of tears is long-since dry;
'Tis only he whose heart has known the deeps
Where loneliness and hopeless shadows lie;

'Tis only he, I say, whose eye is bright
For beauty to which other eyes are blind—
Who knows life's thrill, the wonder of the world,
The fragrance borne upon the summer wind;

'Tis he alone who hears the music sweet
Which fills the air with beauty—throbs and sings;
For only he whose heart has suffered most
Can feel the joy that lies in little things.

Broken

The lute is silent, and I cannot mend
    Its broken string;
The bird has fallen, and I cannot bind
    Its broken wing;
The bow is useless, for I cannot send
    A broken dart;
My voice is silent, for I cannot sing
    A broken heart.

A Moment

I heard the children in the park today.
    I was afar;
I could not see them, but their shouts were gay—
    They always are.
I knew they skated where we did, before
    You went away;
And I would give my all, if you and I
    Could be as they.

To a Rose

Mute witness of a love that once was mine,
Pale, faded petals, once so velvet soft,
And glowing richly with life's vivid hue,
Brown, withered leaves, once fresh and glossy green
Which at my touch dissolve in ashy dust—
What message have you for my lonely heart?
That you were once as beautiful as love,
As fragrant as the gladness of my heart,
And now, like love and gladness, you have died.
But you have fragrance still—my heart has nought.

Hidden Thorns

I plucked a glowing rosebud from its stem—
It grew apart, by summer breezes fanned,
A velvet-petaled, sweetly perfumed queen—
I plucked it—and a rose thorn pierced my hand.

I picked my little kitten up from play—
A tiny ball of fur so soft and sleek,
With purring voice, and velvet-padded paws;
I stroked her—and her sharp claws tore my cheek.

I snatched at love when it was offered me—
A love of hope, all innocent of art,
A joyful love, a dream of love too glad—
I snatched it—and it almost broke my heart.

A Dream and Its Fulfillment

Before I knew you, Lad, I dreamed a dream.
That was the time when I was sad at heart,
Because I loved and was not loved in turn,
And so I wept that we must be apart—

I dreamed that I was walking hand in hand
With someone whom I did not recognize—
A man to whom my heart was bound by love,
Who smiled at me and worshipped with his eyes.

As on I went, with half-reluctant feet—
My heart was ready, but my step was slow—
I did not watch his face; I turned away,
As if I did not really wish to go.

And ever backward cast my wistful eyes
To where another stood—my Boy—the lad
Whom I had loved, and loved in vain so long.
He watched me always and his face was sad.

With arms outstretched, and wistful, hungry eyes,
He gazed and gazed till I was lost to view.
My heart was glad for him I walked beside,
But for my Boy my heart was sorry, too.

And when I woke I could not understand
How I could ever dream so strange a thing;
But mem'ry kept the picture clear for me,
And many times I fell to wondering.

I wondered if I'd ever love again,
And if I did, if Boy would really care;
I strove to call to mind that other's face,
But did not even know if he were fair.

And then you came into my life and smiled,
And worshipped me with wondrous eyes of blue.
I turned—their magic beauty thrilled my heart,
So I could not forget the look of you.

And slowly then my half-reluctant heart
Responded to the wonder of your spell,
And, half-afraid, I gave my love to you,
Yet loved my Boy at first almost as well.

And so my dream came true and, hand in hand,
I went with you and left my Boy behind
To grieve when I was lost; to wish perhaps
That he had understood and not been blind.

The dream that I had dreamed came true, my Lad;
And with the years its memory cannot fade;
But for that glad fulfillment of my dream,
My heart in pain has paid and paid and paid.

Two Nights
(December 7, 1917)

The night before you went away, beloved Laddie mine,
I lay within your arms for hours and watched the firelight
    shine.
You held me close against your heart in silence and
    content;
No need of words between us two—our souls were
    eloquent.

The night before you went away was sweet with love's
    glad pain:
I wept for parting loneliness, but 'twas an April rain.
You kissed me gently in good night, I smiled a last
    goodbye,
And trusting in your love, my heart was too content to
    sigh.

The night was soft and still, my lad, when you returned
    to me.
Close, close against your bursting breast I lay in ecstasy—
An ecstasy of sweet desire, an agony of pain
The flame of passion in my heart, and madness in my
    brain.

You hid your face within my hair; you kissed my mouth
    of flame;
We laughed in wild defiance of our overwhelming shame.
The stinging teardrops mingled on our burning cheeks,
    and dried.
You left my life forever—and the heart within me died!

Away from Home

I'm lonesome for my little room tonight;
This room is big and strange with noisy din.
I miss my pictures, smiling down at me
In quiet with the moonbeams shining in.

I'm lonesome for my little bed tonight;
This bed is big and high, and strange and new.
I want my own soft bed, so comfy warm,
Where I can muss and pull the clothes askew.

I'm lonesome for my brothers dear tonight;
I want to kiss them, and I want my Dad
To come and fix my window, and to lean
Above my bed, and kiss, and make me glad.

I'm all alone—I hate to creep in bed,
There are so many things, somehow, I miss—
My home, my brothers, and my Daddy dear,
But most of all, my mother's goodnight kiss.

To a Boy Who Died

(during an influenza epidemic)

His was no heroic figure:
Very short, and far too fat
To be drafted for a soldier;
But he wasn't glad of that;

For he had the heart and spirit
In his pudgy, comic frame,
Though he could not wear the khaki;
Could not win a fighter's fame.

So he did the best he could do:
Volunteered and went away.
"Limited" they called his service—
But he lost his life today.

And I think, though earthly records
Will not keep his bit for fame,
That somewhere among God's heroes
There's a page that bears his name.

Part Eight
Just Poems

The Old Year and the New

Last night the old year went away,
And when the morning came
I heard the merry New-Year bells,
And things were not the same.

Last night I watched the old year go,
And thought of all it brought,
Of what the year had meant to me,
And all that it had taught—

To bear a new unhappiness;
To bear a stranger thrill;
To understand my weaknesses;
To listen—and be still.

It gave me loves I did not wish;
Took one of them away;
It brought my old love back to me,
Yet kept us parted—aye—

It gave me shame and bitterness,
And loneliness and tears;
It granted me sweet friendliness,
And love for future years.

It taught my lips to laugh again;
And brought my heart the smile
That I had lost the year before
For such a weary while.

It brought my soul content and peace,
And surging back to me
Came love of life, and love of love,
And love of ecstasy.

Last night I watched the old year out,
And watched the new year in,
And thought of all that was to be,
With all that might have been.

A year has gone—a year has come—
The bells are ringing gay—
But will the new year give me joy
Ere it shall pass away?

Or will the new year bring me grief?
Or will it bring me shame?
A year has come—a year has gone—
And nothing's quite the same!

Going to Sleep

Drowsy sleep is o'er me creeping;
Warm and cozy is my bed;
Restful is the downy pillow,
Cool beneath my tired head.

Fresh night wind my cheek is brushing,
Bearing perfume of the rose;
Velvet darkness now enfolds me;
Gently, softly eyelids close.

Rustling whispers, soft night noises
Reach me in my downy nest;
Sweetest languor o'er me stealing—
Oh, the luxury of rest!

The Return

I shut my chest of memories,
    And locked it fast one day;
I tossed the key into the sea,
    And threw the chest away.

But ere the sun had gone to rest,
    Despite the lock and key,
My memories old, a hundredfold,
    Came trooping back to me.

The Land of Yesterdays

My life has been so full of yesterdays!
My mind recalls them now from out the past—
Those dear, dead days of wonder memories,
Of joy and pain too deeply lived to last.

I cherish every hour that has gone by,
And live in thought anew its joy or pain;
I dream old dreams, and think forgotten things,
And vision "might-have-beens" that were in vain.

I love again, and live again, and thrill,
To feel the wonder of the happy past;
I weep again, and sigh again, and wish
That dreams so bright need not to fade so fast.

My life is very rich with what has been!
My heart has lost the Land of Yesterday,
But in my mind it lives forevermore—
That wonder time can never pass away.

Serenity

I have had so much of life,
If the future barren be
I shall fill the empty days
From my store of memory.

I can dry tomorrow's tears
With the laughter of today,
Lost Love's sweetness, lingering,
Driving bitterness away.

Sorrow visits each in turn;
On a day I shall be sad;
But no fate can take from me
All the happiness I've had.

Always Roses

Sometimes my tired feet have climbed all day
And when night fell the summit still was far,
But there were always roses on my way
And through the dark at least one shining star.

No thornless blossoms these; but without fears
I plucked and held them to my eager breast;
And if at times my bleeding hands brought tears
To tired eyes—I still was richly blest.

My soul was fed on beauty through each day;
And fragrance rose from every dusty clod;
For always roses grew along my way;
Friendship, and Sweetness, and the Love of God.

Rebellion

Upon the dance floor Youth holds sway,
And here, in solemn rows,
The staidly prideful mothers watch
Their children prance and pose.
I sit—a rebel—in their ranks,
With wistful, tapping toes.

My son and daughter nod to me;
I smile a gay return;
My heart leaps to the throbbing drums,
And crowding mem'ries burn;
I would be dancing, dancing, too—
But I must sit—and yearn.

Those gay young things, how they would laugh
To know my inward strife.
These placid women sitting here
With no such dreams are rife.
But oh, my heart—my rebel heart—
'Twill not be done with life!

High Heart

I shall be young as long as my eager soul
Stands tiptoe on the threshold of each new day
Questing adventure; crying, "Come what may,
So long as it is Life—for Life is good."

So long as my heart sings
And my spirit has wings
I shall be young.

I shall never grow old, till the day is no longer a challenge,
But only a day in an endless series of days;
When my heart, grown numb, longs only for quiet ways,
And furled are the wings of my spirit that flew so high.

When I seek a place by the fire,
And peace is my one desire,
I shall be old—and die.

Chat with the Devil

Satan perched upon my chair,
Laughed in hellish glee—
"Little did you think, my lass,
You'd belong to me;

Gay the steps your feet have danced;
Sweet the cup you drink,
But the Piper must be paid
Sooner than you think.

What? You say you've done no wrong,
Only dreamed of sin?
Foolish child! That's just the way
All my slaves begin.

Thought is father to the deed
(Mother to it, too)
I can wait a day—a year—
I'll be seeing you!"

On Growing Old

My jaw line is sagging,
　My curls growing gray;
(My pretty brown bonnet
　Must be laid away.)

The frown lines and laugh lines
　Are fixed in their place;
There's no doubt that Time
　Has done things to my face.

But here in my heart
　There's a smile and a song;
The future still beckons
　Me gaily along.

These signs of life's passing
　Don't matter a whit,
So long as my spirit
　Keeps reasonably fit.

Polly-Anne and I
(July 1917)

Oh, my foot is in the stirrup and my hand is on the rein,
And the wind is sporting gaily with my horse's dusky
mane,
While the joy of life is singing on my heartstrings as I ride,
And the pulse of life is thrilling in my horse's even stride;
For we're off upon a holiday, my Polly-Anne and I,
Just to find enchanted palaces where Sleeping Beauties
lie,
And to follow up enchanted paths, that lead we don't
know where:
To a picket fence, a robin's nest, perhaps a dragon's lair.
So it's up the hill and down the hill and round the teasing
bend,
At a canter in our eagerness to see the journey's end;
Then it's on again at flying pace to clear the hindering
bars,
As if Polly-Anne were Pegasus, amounting to the stars.
There's the play of rippling muscles 'neath the pressure
of my knee,
And the breath of woodland balsam drifts adown the
breeze to me,
As it brushes by my glowing cheek, and whips my
loosened hair;
For we're off upon a holiday—and all the world is fair.

Womanhood
(September 1917)

Ripe am I and ready for the hand of love to pluck me,
Ready for the heart of love to come and claim its own,
Is there none to understand, and answer to my calling?
"Here am I!" I whisper, but I find myself alone.

Soft and thick my shining hair, and perfumed for love's
    fondling;
All alight my eager eyes to meet an answering flame;
Full and red my hungry lips, and sweet for love's
    caressing;
Pulsing warm my velvet cheek with passion's happy
    shame;

Smooth and soft my hands to clasp and cling in love's
    delighting;
Young my eager body, with its passion-pulse aglow;
Full of longing life my heart, and hungry with desiring—
Ripe am I and ready—Is there none to see or know?

The Skeptic

In books the hero always finds
    The lovely heroine,
And fate, though fickle, always smiles,
    And lets young Cupid win.
But when it comes to living—Life
    Has not so bright a gleam,
And "happy ever after" is
    A kind of hopeless dream.

In movies men are Grecian gods
    And girls coquettish queens.
They sigh into each other's eyes,
    And love—upon the screens.
But when it comes to living—Love
    Is often strangely slow.
Romance is an elusive thing
    I never chanced to know.

Home

Home! There's a blessed comfort in that word.
One little syllable that whispers rest,
That sighs a lullaby of love and friends,
Of peace, contentment, everything that's best.

Home! It's strange how very dear you are.
Each well-remembered scene delights my eyes;
Each nook and cranny holding mem'ries dear,
Refills my soul with tender, glad surprise.

Home! There's a sweet contentment in that word.
Which spells for me the world I hold most dear.
Be still, my restless heart, and find yourself,
And join my restless soul in quiet here.

Philosophy

How fast time flies! We cannot keep
One little hour that hurries by;
It comes, it goes—and we're of those
Who've one hour less before they die.

The fleet days speed into the past;
We cannot check their hurried flight.
Too swift by far the days that are
Become the days that were delight.

Then do not wish your time away
In longings for the days to be,
But live today as best you may,
And love the past for memory.